T0196371

DEATH
WHAT IS IT

DEATH
WHAT IS IT

REV. LEROY WRIGHT JR.

authorHOUSE®

AuthorHouse™
1663 Liberty Drive
Bloomington, IN 47403
www.authorhouse.com
Phone: 1-800-839-8640

Published by AuthorHouse   06/29/2013

ISBN: 978-1-4817-5826-0 (sc)
ISBN: 978-1-4817-5824-6 (e)

Library of Congress Control Number: 2013909924

DEATH
WHAT IS IT

Some scriptures were quoted without references, some were with references. They all came from the King James version.

Genesis 3: 19
1 Corinthians 15:55
Matthew 28:18
Exodus 12:23
1 Kings 17: 21-22
2 Kings 4:34
John 11:42
Isaiah 11:6-7
Genesis 4: 1-2
Psalm 82: 16
Luke 16: 19-31
Revelation 6: 9-10
Genesis 2:7
Ephesians 6
Exodus 15:9
Genesis 3: 16
Job 38
John 3: 11-12
      15:26
      16: 13-14
Genesis 1: 11-12

Death What Is It

Death, what is it? Why are there so many people out there so afraid of it? The same question can be asked. Why are there so many out there who want to go to heaven, but don't want to die? Why is it so hard for some believe to accept death when it comes into our lives? Could it be because we don't want to accept what God told our first father Adam, after he disobeyed him in the garden? In Genesis 3: 19. It says: In the sweat of thy face shalt thou eat bread, till thou return unto the ground; for out of it wast thou taken: for dust thou art, and unto dust shalt thou return.

Did you hear or received that in your spirit? God said! He knows where we come from. How long on this earth we will live, and how long we shall remain in the grave, before he returns to receive the church unto him self. Maybe someone could help me or explain why we as believers in Christ, don't really understand God when he is speaking so clear and plain.

I will give my opinions, later. Hopefully some will come to realize that I understand God in ways, that others may have never thought of. You see, death use to be a real threat. At one time it was a very dangerous and hurting threat toward man kind. It use to sting.

When we as christians die, we should not have any fear. Jesus our father, the son of the living God: has taken the sting out of death and the victory away from the grave. 1 Corinthians 15:55. All power on earth and in heaven has been given unto him. Matthew 28:18. No I have never died nor as some would say, had an out of body experience. But I did experience my body going numbed. I went to bed before my decease wife and as I was lying there. The left side of my body began to lose all feeling. My entire left side, from my foot to my shoulder. As I prayed, I even began wondering what would happen if I had not been able to call on the name of Jesus.

Death is a spirit, an angle: (Exodus 12:23 speaks of him as the destroyer), and it used to have full control over it victims. It is a cross over from this physical life to the spiritual life. In the days of the old, when someone died, it was all over, unless they had enough faith in God to use the old prophets to pray and lay hand on the love one that died. Elijah cried out unto the Lord three time before the soul of the Zarephath woman, son spirit, returned back to his body. (1Kings 17:21-22). Elisha also lay upon the son of the of the Shunammite woman. (2 Kings 4:34). He also had to pray to the Lord.

When Jesus raised Lazarus from the grave, it was used to prove to the people that were standing around, that he was the son of God. (John 11:42). All these people had to die again. Jesus was and had to be the first and only one to rise from the grave, never to die again.

Let me see if I can explain death this way. From the beginning there was no death. Where did he come from, God knows because he created him. There was no need for him because no one or any animal died. Man could walk up to and pet a lion or bear. Lions at one time did not eat meat, they ate straws, grass. (Isaiah 11:6-7). Snakes stood like men and could speak the same language. Oh no they didn't you may say, how do you think Eve understood what was said, when the serpent told her she would not die, if she ate of the forbidden tree? He told her she would not die, but would become as gods. Which by the way, we are gods, if you didn't know this. (Psalm 82:6). When she ate of the tree of knowledge, good and evil, nothing happen, but when she gave it to Adam, he ate, then and only then, they knew they were naked. Their eyes became open, which brings me to this question. Before they ate of the tree, good and evil, were they walking around with there eyes close, totally depending upon God for everything? I am not even going to touch that or try explaining it. Before Adam ate of the forbidden tree, the tree of good and evil, the tree of knowledge, nothing died. It was not until the trust between God and man had been broken, that death came into play. Why or what kind of death came into play you may ask? It was a spiritual death, that separated man from God. Adam did not die the physical death, but was put out of the garden. If God would have left him in the garden, then he would have eaten of the tree of life and never would have died. This would have given them the power to commit sin in the present of God any time they wanted to, and that could not happen. It was then, animals began to kill and eat other animal. It was not until then, after being put out of the garden that Adam knew Eve sexually. (Genesis chapter 4). He didn't gave her a name until they were about to be put out of the garden. (Genesis 3:20). In the garden he called her woman, but after the committing of sin, he called her Eve. When he went into her, she became pregnant and give birth to a son and called him Cain. He was a tiller of the ground. He went into her again and she gave birth to A'bel, a keeper of sheep. Now the boys grew and offered God an offering. Because Cain refuse to give God his best, and A'bel did, he became angry when God refused to except his offering. He became so angry that he slew his brother A'bel. This was the first physical murder, the first sin of man shedding the blood of another man. The first fugitive of mankind with a bounty, on his head. Isn't it a shame when man do evil to someone else, he want someone else to have mercy on him. It was after the killing of Able, death went on a rampage, causing all kind of trouble. A man's blood cries out to God for justice when it spilled out onto the earth. Many men were born, and many died, before God got enough of man's sin. God tried for one hundred twenty years, preaching through Noah, to get man to turn his life around and come back to him. Because of sin, death laid in wait, waiting to capture and hold as many disobedient souls as possible. All those who trust and believed in God, when their spirit left the body, it went into the bosom of Abraham. Those who don't, their souls was and is still taken to hell. Where do you think the rich man who refuse to give Lazarus the crumbs that fell from his table went? He described it as a place of tormented and in flames. His spirit and soul was not dead and could still see in the spirit world, and could still talk. (Luke 16:19-31). Everyone needs to listed to the preachers. All these people going around talking about they are seeing human's spirits in old houses, or haunted houses. You should listen to what I am saying to you. When the soul leave the body it goes to one out of two places. Under the altar in heaven (Revelation 6: 9-10) or hell, Luke 16. That what they are playing with it is very dangerous. Those are falling angels, cast out of heaven by Michael and his angels. Read Revelation chapter 12 for yourself if you don't believe what I am telling you. No human spirit or soul can wonder around on this earth with out a body to live in. God did not blow his spirit out into nothing, but into the dust they made man and he became a living soul. (Genesis 2: 7). The bible tells us of the great dragon who was cast out, that old serpent, called the Devil, and Satan, which deceiveth the whole world: he was cast out into the earth, and his angels were cast out with him. What those people are dealing with are demons, not the spirit of humans. If God would have done that, you and I would not have to use doors or cars to go through or go anywhere. But I know some of the people in the world we live in today, are looking for something because they have been deceived by the enemy. Paul said in Ephesians 6, beware of the tricks of the fallen angles, by putting on the whole armor of God. It is the reason Adam fell in the garden. It was promised to God that he, the enemy, he would do everything in his power to destroy mankind, (Exodus 15:9) spoken through Pharaoh in his anger. The enemy said: I will purse, I will overtake, I will divide the spoil, my lust shall be satisfied up on them; I will draw my sword, my hand shall destroy them. There are all kind of people out there, and they do not believe that God is real. Believe me, and those who have a personal relationship with him, trust him and total depend on him. We can say JESUS IS LORD, this is something no demons can say or admit. But they will deceive mankind and cause him to say there is no God, or I don't believe in God. They are lost and will lose their life if they don't wise up and accept Jesus as Lord.

This bring me to the spiritual death. The spiritual death is being separated from God. Those people can be found all over this world. They can even be found in the church. Some go to church, because there parents make them go. They have no interest in what the preacher has to say. There is nothing that he can say to convince, convict, or persuade them, to turn there life over to God. But if he is preaching and teaching the gospel, and not sugar coating it, the word of God itself has power unseen. The word will convince, convict and persuade them to change there lives. Then there are those who do believe that God exist but will not admit that he is God and God all by himself. They can not accept the fact that one can be three. They have no understanding how something can be so perfect. You will never hear them say the name of Jesus. They try finding all type of excuses not to believe that there is a God. They can not see for believing that he didn't created this world and everything in it. Some try explaining things this way, the big bang theory. It was a big bang all right. Think people, things that collide into each other cause damage. If it was a big bang, tell me why a peach tree can not grow banana's, or a fish can not give birth to dogs. When God finish speaking his most holiest and precious words, he stood back and said all is very good. (Genesis 1:31). Everything was in its right place and right form. Pecan trees can only bring forth pecans, fig trees figs and apple trees apples. All of his creations brought forth offspring's of it's kind. Male and female were separated and to this day, and until Jesus return, only females will be able to give birth. No male can give birth to a baby. That is the word of God and all ways will be the word of God. It was his rapture to woman kind as a punishment for the sin commit in the garden. When they were casted out, God told Eve that (Genesis 3:16) I will greatly multiply your sorrow and your conception: in pain you shall bring forth children: your desire shall be for your husband, and he shall rule over you. These are the words of God that show me how foolish some women and men can really be. "They say I don't need a man, I can make it all by myself." If I was standing before one of these women, in the most respectable way that I can, I would ask her how do you think you got here on this earth? Your mother did not sleep with another woman to become pregnant. She slept with a male and that is the only way she could become pregnant. Plus, if it was not the will of God at that time, your mother would have never gotten pregnant. Life come from God, not from another human being. He is the giver and sustainer of life, not man. Tell me this, can a man ride on the wind, or tell which way it is coming from before it hit him in the face? Can a man form a cloud in the sky or hang a star in the sky? Here is something he asked Job, hath the rain a father? Who hath begotten the drops of dew? Out of whose whom came the ice? And the hoary frost of heaven, who hath gendered it? There is a lot more, read Job chapter 38. So don't ever think you know what is best for you and that you don't need a man. Women will always need men, and then man still can not stop death from coming to himself nor woman. It does not matter where you are when death come for you. If you are on the east coast and death is on the west coast, when your time is up, you have to leave this world. Now the biggest and the most important question you will have to answer before leaving this side: where do you want to spend eternity, heaven or hell? It's your choice, but make no mistake about it, death is on it's way. You have a choice to suffer and go through a hard death, or the one that Jesus has taken the sting and power out of.

This bring us to the physical death. Oh the physical death. Take a look around you, at the people around you, even on your job, no matter what the conversation they never ever say anything about God? How many of them make that ignorant statement in the morning when you say good morning to them: what's so good about it? They curse the morning, curse the heat, curse the rain, curse the winter, they curse each and everything that God do. My question and statement to them is, if you don't like what God is doing, why don't you trying skipping one day? Try not waking up one morning. If you don't like what God is doing, I can guarantee you, you sure will not like what Satan can do to you. Think about this, what happen to you when everything that you try to do, go wrong? That is one of the times you want to blame God for your troubles. But you forgot, you don't have a connection to God. You acknowledge Satan in just about everything you do or say. You give him praise when you see another mans woman and she looks good to you. Even when one of your children make you use words toward them. You are suppose to love them but, that goes out the window when they use what has been given to them by God, a mind of there own to think. What is that you say, don't make me beat your backside, I will knock the hell, out of you. Sit your backside over there and you bet not move. You get on my got water fall nerves. You make me so sick, I can just beat your backside. You are so stupid, you got that on your daddy's side. Here is one you are suppose to do anyway. I will beat the hell out of you. Now the bible tell us to spare not the rod, it will not kill your child, but would drive there soul away from hell. (Proverbs 23:14). It doesn't mean that hell is in your child, just sinful ways. It's a shame so many parents are setting their off springs up for death to take them to hell. Death rejoices because you never teach your children about God, but from your own mouth, with your own mouth, you teach them how to praise Satan. No you don't you say. How many times have you told your child that you love them since they have reached the age to really understand what is going on. I know some mothers, show all kind of love toward there babies as long as he or she can not speak back to them. If they could really understand baby talk, they would probably start spanking the child before he or she could speak clear enough to be understood. A child picks up things they hear other people say. They don't know how to curse or tell lies, they get it from you. You are the one who they first get to know before knowing anyone else. They clink to your voice, smell and sound. They trust and depend upon you mothers, for everything they need. If you never teach them how to love and forgive because you never do it, than how do you expect them, to know how to love and forgive? You have the most precious time in there life, because you are mom, you are dad. Don't you realize that God trusted you with a part of himself? He is the one who put that life in you and it became a living soul. So will you try to teach your baby how to live not only on this side, but to get prepared to live on the other side also? A life that is lived on this side, separated from God, die and go to hell on the other side, is one that has not been worth living. It is so easy to love, and forgive, if you are connected to the true vine, being Jesus himself. You don't look at a man's skin color and judge him, but you look at the God in him, if the both of you know and accept Jesus as Lord.

Now for the ones who has accept, confessed and have been born again. You should know that you are now the light of this world, that's because you are still in this world. We, you and I, have a work to do. It was given to us on the day Jesus ascended back into heaven, he said (Matthew 28-19-20). Go ye therefore, and teach all nations, baptizing them in the name of the Father, and of the Son, and of the Holy Ghost: teaching them to observe all things whatsoever I have commanded you and lo I am with you always, even unto the end of the world. I find it hard sometimes that we as christians, forget that people watch us closer than we think. What we do or say when we are not around people that know we are christians, can be seen through our children. Yes they will pick up things from other children but we as moms and dads, should have the biggest influence over our children. Please don't be fooled by what you see and hear them do. They watch and hear things said about you if you are an active member in the church. They pick up on things said about you in specials programs at the church. They may hear how well you teach the Sunday school lessons, or sing in the choir, or pray, or give special speeches, than go home and raise hell at your wife or husband. They also listen and learn from their Sunday school teacher that life and death is in the power of the tongue. (Proverbs 18:21). How many people in your church have they heard you and your wife cutting down, because they didn't do things, the way you though they should? How many times have they listened to you talk on the phone about someone, like the pastor, or minister, or another deacon or member? When will we as pastors, ministers, ministers of music and other body heads of the church realize, that the people we judge or look down upon, is no better than we once were? We to were some kind of a sinner, some still are. Someone took the time to help and teach us. They didn't force their ways or thoughts on us but allowed God to shape and remold us. What make us think we can shape people into what we want them to be? They are not serving us but God, the same one that called us. We can not call a man or woman by the heart with a silence peaceful voice. But God can, he called you and I and we, those without any doubt are still praising him today. I know this because of some of the things that happen in my life. I am a minister who know without a shallow of a doubt, know that I have been called by God to preach and teach his word. Some ministers have tried to give me their opinion about something while trying to teach the Sunday school lesson. I have been passed over when it come to preaching, or leading songs in the choir. Lies have been spread about me, from some ladies, because they could not change me to be what they though I should be. I and others, have realize that no matter what we do, someone will always think the worst of us. As children of God, we often forget that we are all in this walk of life together. No one is greater than the other. We are all born and shaped in the iniquity of sin. We all have fallen and come short of the glory of God. Not one of us can give anyone salvation. Salvation comes from God. At this point some may think or say yes I can. Then tell us this, who save you? Who called you out of sin? What heaven or hell do you have to put those who accept or reject Jesus? Would you give your off spring to die for the people of this world? No you would not. You would be unjust, unfair, and selfish one. Why do I say that, you might ask? How may people in your life you do not like? How often do you drive down the freeway and want to give someone a piece of your mind? I think you need that little piece of mind for yourself. When death comes, and he will come, you may need that and a whole lot more, depend on how or what happened, when he do come. We as Christians should have some type of understanding that death is only a part of life, yet so many still don't want to accept that it is a promise from Jesus himself. Remember the statement,(John 14:3). And if I go away and prepare a place for you, I will come again and receive you unto myself, that where I am, there ye may be also. If we as Christians understand this, why is it that when we loose a love one, we carry on like we have lost the only friend in the world? What is Jesus? I thought he was the one we trusted when trouble comes. I know we will go through some suffering, but the scripture said, he will never put on us more than we can bear. Why not cast this down at his feet and let him carry us through this point and time of life? Everyone want to go to heaven, but no one want to be touched by the enemy. In spite of any and everything that the enemy bring our way in life, God has already given us everything we need to go through life. Whether it is in good health or sickness, you should know this if you have read Ephesians one and understand it. He is the bridge to glory land, and Jesus is the driver, the healer, the way, the truth and the light, on this side and on the other side. He keeps us alive on this side, and he will give us the eternal life on the other side. All of this is in the plans of God himself. He is the one that loves us so much that he has given the most enter part of himself. His one and only begotten son, not yours or mines, because we can't or couldn't be pure or righteous enough to forgive or love all mankind, regardless of what he or she does. The only thing that God will not forgive mankind for is blaspheming against the Holy Spirit. Now do you think your or my son could take what Jesus went through? What about that loved one someone kills, those people who allowed themselves to make this statement. I will never forgive you, or you can die and go to hell. How hard would it be for you to forgive someone who kill your small child, or rape your son or daughter? What I can say is the same thing Jesus said on the cross, Father, forgive them for they know not what they do. Maybe not from the beginning but after having time to think. Someone need to think, the same word that come out of a person's mouth, comes back to them. If we can't say something good or positive about someone, keep quiet. Don't say anything, do what God said to Moses, stand still and see the salvation of the Lord. Let God take care of it. It may seem as if he or she is getting away with something but be patience. You don't know how to apply enough pain, or be affective enough to really hurt them. God know how, when and where to hit them, that he would get there attention. He has ways that we have never though of. Death is something that has been used by God ever since he destroyed the world with water. It is also the last thing he will cast into the lake of fire. Things will be the same way or better than the first because there will be no need for death anymore. Once Christ come back to receive the church unto himself, nothing will ever die again. There will be no need for the sun, nor candle, darkness will never be know again. The only light will be that of the Lord God himself. There will be no crying, no death, no sorrow or pain. All of the thing of this world will be destroyed, that is the fire that the Lord will destroy this world with. There will be some children, that will not make it, some parents who will not make it. Then there will be some mothers and fathers along with there children, who will make it, but they will not be there as fathers, mothers, and children. They will be there as children or sons of God. There will be no female or males in the kingdom of God. There will be no need for reproduction. The only marriage will be that of God and his people. So if your mother or father never tell you anything about Christ, you need to accept Jesus as your Lord and saviour, believe it in your heart, that God has raised him from the dead and he is now sitting at the right hand of the Father in Heaven. Please do not let anyone brain wash you into believing that God does not exist. What ever you do, you make sure your name is written down in the Book of Life. That is a guarantee that you will have a chance to the tree of life forever and ever.

Now I said I would give my opinion on how or what I think or feel in trying to describe God. I know that I am not the only one that has sat back and observed the way he does things. He knew what and how he wanted things from the beginning or before the beginning of this world or mankind. He made mankind for his pleasure. It was with the dust of the earth in creation, they kneeled down and decided to make something for themselves. It would be called mankind. He would be in the image and likeness of them. Man, he had no help mate, so they put man to sleep and took a rib from his body and made woman. They in term gave them everything that they would ever need to live and be happy in the garden. It was not until after the sin of mankind, that God spoke the words, be fruitful and multiply. Now watch this, in the term of multiplying, everything in his creation is still the same today. Nothing has changed. An apple tree is still bringing forth apples, banana still bring fort bananas, peach and so on. But here is something they all have in common. They can be seen all over the world. Whether it be in paper, or chairs, table or other furniture. From that day to this day, everything that can be seen or unseen is being held together through and by his son, Jesus the Christ. No matter what he created, in all of his creation, he gave his son to only one of his creation. There is nothing in his creation that he love so much that he would give his only begotten son to and for. That is mankind. Some people has never given any thought to what was said in Jesus pray to his father. He said all that you have given me I have kept. I have lost none but the son of prediction. I PRAY NOT FOR THIS WORLD, said Jesus. Some may call me wrong when I say, I don't pray for this world. I understand that when Jesus return, he is not coming back for this world, he is coming back for the people in this world. Those who have confessed and believed on him. This world, his creation will be destroyed by fire, because it is contaminated with sin. I pray for the people in this world, that God will continually keep us. I pray for those who has heard his voice and accept Jesus as Lord and Saviour. I also pray for those who reject Jesus and that they will one day have enough time to come to him as there Savoir. Why should I worry over something that God himself is not worrying over? I can not change it or do anything to make it better. I am more into what will happen to those who do not accept Jesus, as Lord and Saviour. It is import to me because no matter what Satan or man do or try to do to me or you in this body, he can never ever touch the soul. God and only God can destroy both body and soul.

Let us take a short and brief look at those who are on the road to death. They are the ones who live life with no conviction or conscious. No matter how you try to tell them that dealing drugs, could bring them to a short life. They could be killed or sent to prison for doing things against the law. Getting caught can take away their freedom and put them in the place where they would loose everything. They maybe put in the position and have to kill or be killed in prison. Then there are those who live on the outside of prison, shacking up woman with woman or man with man, or man and woman. All of these are a sin in the eyes of God. Man living with man or woman with woman is a sure way to go straight to hell. Why do you think Sodom and Gomorrah was destroyed. Man living with a woman unmarried can also lead to destruction? Scripture said, it is better to marry than to burn. Many people know they are headed to destruction but just refuse to turn their life around. So many think they have time to live like they want and that they have tomorrow to change. Who told them that? Who told them that they have tomorrow or will live to see tomorrow? How often do young men and women get into fights and one of them lose there life? How many young men or ladies have lost there life, just walking down the sidewalk of a street. How many have lost there lives because they were caught with another man's wife or woman husband. If there are any children, they are the ones who lose. Mom or dad is dead and mom or dad goes to prison for life. How many of these talk show host would go off the tv, if the younger people would live according to the standards of God. I pray that someday some of them would see themselves on the tv and how ridiculous they really seems. Fathers and mothers looking ridiculous because they refuse to put the belt on there backside when they should have. Now they want to go on tv to try getting help for their children when they should have gone to the church for God's help. Fathers or mothers bring boyfriend or girlfriend into there home and he or she goes after there children. Those are some of the seeds that was sown on bad ground. Then there are those who tell there seeds that they should not get married. Man what kind of a stumbling block parent are they. Telling their child they can go straight to hell, indirectly. Think about it, (Proverbs chapter 7), tell us if a man see a woman, who is trying to get him into her bed, turn and go the other way. The way she is leading him, the end is destruction. Women should look at this in the same way. We all have a chance to do what's right in the sight of God. It is our chance to plant the seed of God into each and every one of our children, before they make the wrong choices in life. Each and everyone has a chance to plant seeds into good ground. God will not force himself on no one. He is still standing at the door of each one who has not excepted him, waiting for them to open and let him in. Then and only then will he come in and sup with them. (Revelation 3:20). When he has enough of man rejecting him, he will just remove his hand and death will come. That's when disobedient children want to call on the Lord. They want to cry out why them, why not somebody else? Why not them, now is the time you should cry, knowing that they died in sin, there soul is lost forever. Now those who die in Christ is not dead but only sleeping. Which is best to die in Christ and live forever, or die in sin to burn and suffer in hell forever and ever? That's one of the reason I pray that, those fools who think man and man or woman and woman could get married. That's not in the will of God. No man can plant his seed into another man and have a child or women in woman. GOD told man and woman to be married, not Cain and Abel. Now do you get the picture. Now here is God in a more earthly form. Have you read or heard about the man who went out to sow. Earthly term, plant seeds for his crop. He cast out his seeds and they fell in many different spots. Some fell on stony places, some among thorns, some by the wayside and some on good ground. They all died, or was eaten by birds because there was something wrong with the place of sowing. It was not deep enough or too shallow because of the stones. They fell in the place where grass would grow up and over take the plant, and choke it out. This farmer did not put much into his field to get the best of crops. Just a reminder, be fruitful and multiply. Now in today time, farmers purchases larger tractors to work and prepare there fields before planting his seeds. He put whatever chemicals needed to kill the weeds that may come up and choke out his crops. In term he puts down fertilizer to make sure the seed have what ever it need to produce as much of whatever as possible. Lets use corn as the plant. Sometimes the grain of corn is treated with certain chemicals to stop the bugs and birds from eating it. Once it is put into the ground, that grain of corn must die before it can start growing and break the ground, coming into a world of unknown. Once it has broken the earth and start growing, the farmer will work his field to keep down grass, given his plant a chance to grow and produce two, three or sometime four ears of corn on one stalk. That is what's know as a good crop, when that one grain of corn produce that many ears. Now that one grain of corn, may bring fort two or three ears of corn. On one of the ears there may be, pick a number, fifty grains of corn. A whole field produce enough to feed many of families. Now when farmers were allowed to plant their whole field, there wasn't a food shortage. Only when the governor got more involved, things really began go down hill, if you know what I mean. You see there is one who was not control by man or Satan. He is the most prosperous farmer I have ever known. No one in this universe can touch or even come close to him. No one could tell him when or where to plant his seed. He used the most pressure seed that could ever be planted. His name is God. The man chopped his field (the earth) to get it ready for planting and God prepared his seed before planting it. Mankind spat on, slap, made fun of, wrongful judge, had a crown of thorns put on his head, beaten him with a whip, stripped of his robe, nailed him to a cross, and yet, man could not kill the seed of God. On the cross, the seed of God still asked his father to forgive that which they told to be fruitful and multiply. On that same cross, he looked up toward heaven and asked his father, why did he forsake him? Yet he never betrayed him or lost trust in his father because he said, into thy hand I commend my spirit. His seed gave up his own life so that we could live forever. His seed die and was planted in the earth. Hey, did you catch that? Did you understand what happen? The seed of God died before he was planted into the earth. The seed that man plant has to die after it is planted into the earth. The seed of God was planted into the same thing man was formed from, dust of the earth. It was in the earth that victory was worn. It was in the earth captures was set free. It was in the earth that the grave and death lost all of there powers. He stayed there in the earth three days and nights and on the third day he rose to never die again. He was given all powers on earth and in heaven. He has brought fort more seeds than any other seed ever planted. Reminder, be fruitful and multiply were the words spoken from God toward his creation. From those holy and obedient word, the earth brought forth that which was yield within itself. (Genesis 1: 11-12). Once again where was man? What was man created from? From that one seed, hundred upon hundred, thousands upon thousands, millions upon, millions, nations upon nations, and a number that no man could count. From that one seed from God, it has gone all over the world, known as Jesus the Christ, know also as the living son of God, and the word of God. So see death has no power over the seed of God, nor do the grave. They both have lost what at one time was power to them. They are now something that is being used by God until he decide to return for his church. Now some one may not agree with the way I see things, but everyone is entitle to his or her own opinion. But to me God is portraying himself in this manner, as a farmer. He is the only one that planted a seed that is still producing to this day. If you are not connected to that vine, Jesus, I pray you get connected. Don't be the branch that is throw into the fire. Don't be the branch that is taken up and cast into the fire to be burned.(John 15:6). Stay connected to Jesus so you may bring fort (green leaves), life instead. You know we all are seed planters, whether you believe it or not. Jesus said the harvest is ready but the labors are few. Every time you tell someone about the word of God, you are planting seeds. The word of God, you plant, God water and give the increase. This field we live in, this world is full of ready harvest. There are so many still out there who want to hear and come to God, but they are afraid because of the people around them. Just a word to those people and I pray you will listen. On judgment day, those who are criticizing you for excepting Jesus as your Lord and Savoir, will also have to go before the judgment seat. That is the judgment seat of God. You may see them or they you, but we all will, and there is no maybe, will give in account for what we do or how we treat others. Regardless how someone looks at you or how they try to judge you, your sin, pass, present and future have been prayed for by the one seed planted by

God. Remember Solomon said if any man like wisdom, let him ask. Satan is wise and we must be aware of his tricks. So why not do what I did. Ask God for spiritual wisdom and spiritual knowledge and spiritual understanding of his word. He will open your eyes to see his word through a different view. Just when the Holy Spirit start teaching you, don't be doubtful of what he is showing you. That's part of his job to show and bring to your remembrance the things about Jesus. But let me warn you ahead of time. There are some out there who will not believe you because they don't understand. Believe me, because there are some fighting me today. I know it is because they haven't become wise enough yet to ask God for what I have. To me I see these people today as the people in the days of old. When Jesus came and start teaching them things of himself, they didn't want to hear him because they were lost and didn't know the scripture as well as they though they did. So don't be surprise when you meet some of them. They have been in church for ten to whatever numbers of years and are still on milk. They can tell you what they have learn but that's as far as they can go. They are the ones who try to teach others and when the Holy Spirit reveal something new, they don't want to hear it. Remember, he told Nicodemus, (John 3:11-12). Verily, verily, I say unto thee, we speak that we do know, and testify that we have seen; and ye receive not our witness. 12. If I have told you earthly things, and ye believe not, how shall ye believe, if I tell you of heavenly things? The bible can't hold all the things about God. You can read his word and the Holy Spirit can reveal something to you that others can't see. He is the true witness. Jesus said in St John 15:26. But when the Comforter is come, whom I will send unto you from the Father, even the Spirit of Truth, which proceedeth from the Father, he shall testify of me. 16: 13-14. Howbeit when he, the Spirit of Truth, is come, he will guide you into all truth: for he shall not speak of himself; but whatsoever he shall hear, that shall he speak: and he will show you things to come. 14. He shall glorify me: for he shall receive of mine, and SHALL SHOW IT UNTO YOU. Only what we do for the kingdom of God will last. But please, be aware of the enemy Satan, and don't let him put things into you mine. Make sure that it is God, that is talking to you. If you are his sheep, you will know his voice, you will know when he is talking to you.

God bless each and everyone of you. Much love. Thank you.

Rev. Leroy Wright Jr.

FROM
THE
SPIRITUAL
SIDE

Scripture are being used from the
King James Bible

2 Timothy 2:15
St John 14:26
Corinthians 2: 9-10
St John 3: 11-12
St John 4: 22-24
Matthew 17: 11-13
Genesis 7: 10
Ezekiel 26: 19
St John 19
Ecclesiastes 12: 7-8
Matthew 4: 16
St John 14: 11
Genesis 2:7
Genesis 2: 6
Exodus 15: 9
Genesis 2: 17
Genesis 2:3
Matthew 2: 11-33
Mark 5: 25-34

From the Spiritual Side

Let me start by getting this out of the way first. I am not an over religious person. I do not consider myself more holier than anyone else, nor consider myself to be a bible scholar, or claim to know everything. Truly, I am not so religious that I can't understand. But there are a few things I am very thankful for, that God has done in my life. One of them is the vision he allowed me to see of New Jerusalem. It has an un-describable beauty of color and pureness. The streets, the walls, the river, the tree of life, the throne and the Spirit of God himself, could never truly be described by man. He really can't bring any justice or bring glory: to God of what Jesus has prepared for those who love him. I am truly thankful that he allowed me to see that in a vision. I have met some people who are so righteous in there self righteous ways, that they think they are right in everything, when it comes to explaining the bible. They have gotten to the point that, because they study the bible every day, according to them, that when you have a conversation with them about the bible, there is no way someone who doesn't read everyday, can get a word in edge wise. Jesus did not force himself down any one's throat. How can we help someone, if we are so forceful pushing the word of God down their throats: without listening to what they are trying to tell us? Stop, listen to what someone is saying before you start preaching to them. They may understand more about the bible than you give them credit for. After listening to them and they don't understand or misinterpret the scripture, then try explaining it correctly to them. You don't want to turn them away before they have a chance to really know Christ. Could this be part of the reason why some members of the church, will not get involve in some programs where they attend? Could there be more church members pastors, than the pastor? I have had the opportunity to meet some brothers ministers, if you listen to them, think they are in the position of the pastor, than the pastor of the church. Some have not gone to bible school, even there, they can only teach you so much, but they try to tell others, what's in the word of God and what's not. Have you ever heard this statement, if it is not in the bible, we don't want to hear it. Before I jump on that statement, let me say this. To me those are people who will limit God in his or her thinking. Now I know the scripture said we should study to show thyself approved unto God (not man, but God, because God share his glory with no man), a workman that needeth not to be ashamed, rightly dividing the word of truth. 2 Timothy 2:15. I also know in revelation that the scripture said that if any man shall add unto these things, God shall add unto him the plagues that are written in this book. And if someone add anything, God will take away his part of the book of life. I look at these people who show signs of not believing what Jesus said: But before the Comforter, which is the Holy Ghost, whom the Father will send in my name, he shall teach you all things, and bring all things to your remembrance, whatsoever I have said unto you. (John 14:26). (16:14). He shall glorify me; for he shall receive of mine; and shall show it unto you. Now if you don't believe that the Holy Spirit can teach someone something you don't know, and you reject what they say before you understand what they are saying, do some research in the scripture for yourself before you cut them down. Don't be so doubtful, because they may be more of a spiritual servant than you; because you believe that if you can not see it, you will not believe what they are saying. They may be able to show you something that God has not shown you through his word. Believe me, I have seen something that others have not, and when I tried showing it to them, they only show me, as Paul said, I would not have your ignorant brothering. Before you shut someone down give them a chance to explain what they are trying to say. What would you do, or how would you feel, if he or she is give the chance to show someone in the scripture: what the holy spirit has revealed unto them. Even if you don't know it, now you do, it is a sin to cut someone off when they are speaking. You do not know what they are going to speak. What if someone is getting ready to tell you that they know the Lord, not in the way that you do, but in his or her own way. If he or she said that he or she walk and talk to God through out the day, and sometimes they can hear the Lord speaking back to them, will you tell them they are wrong. My question to you is, what make you think he or she is not telling the truth? What changed about God? Do you think God has become a mute? You think he only speaks through his word. Just how much do you know about God, if you think this way? Have you ever took the time to pray to God, and he answered your prayers while you are praying? Have he ever answered your prayers and you hear him, that it cause you to stumble in your prayers, because he answered you? Have you ever read in the book of Job how God speaks through the thunder, or how his breath change the seasons? No one will ever make me or convince me that God does not speak into today time. In a case like this, to me that person characterized and limited God in what he can do. They quote the scripture, I can do all things through Christ Jesus who strengthened me; but they limit God. Putting a limit on God show me that you can do only what you can see. This show me that you do not believe everything that the bible says. The scripture said that Enoch walked and talked with God and he was not: for God took him. Would you talk to someone, or a God who will never answer you? If so why would you pray to a god that would not answer you. Your faith is shallow and with a finite mind, you will never get to know some of the things that is hidden in the word of God. Oh yes my friends, just as God hide some things from the people of old, there are still today something in the word of God that we today still don't know. I will explain some of what the Holy Spirit has revealed unto me later. In this, 1 Corinthians 2: 9-10. But as it is written, Eye hath not seen, nor ear heard, neither have entered into the heart of man, the things which God hath prepared for them that love him. 10. But God hath revealed them unto us BY HIS SPIRIT: for the Spirit searcheth all things, yea, the deep things of God. It is not so much that he hide it from us, we can not see it because maybe we have not asked the right question, or maybe it is because we are still seeking God with a carnal mind. That is why we must do what was spoken by Jesus himself. In John 3: 11-12. Verily, verily, I say unto thee, we speak that we do know, and testify that we have seen; and ye receive not our witness.

12. If I have told you earthly things, and ye believe not, how shall ye believe, if I tell you of heavenly things? John 4:22. Ye worship ye know not what: we know what we worship: for salvation is of the Jews. (this mean not us, at that time, meaning gentiles) 23. But the hour cometh, and now is, when the true worshipers shall worship the Father in spirit and in truth: for the Father seeketh such to worship him. 24: God is a Spirit: (hello) and they that worship him must worship him in spirit and in truth. So if you think that God don't speak to us today maybe you still don't understand the scriptures when he said, he that has and ear let him hear what the Spirit saith unto the churches. You are a part of the churches aren't you? Here is a thought for you, when you read your bible, do you ever meditate on the word of God? How deep do you allow yourself to go? This part take faith, how much faith do you have? Do you allow the Holy Spirit to take you places you have never been before? Have you grown spiritual enough to allow the Holy Spirit to take you into the pages of your bible? Have you ever been to Jerusalem in spirit? Have you ever seen yourself watching Jesus and the people of that day while it was taking place? Have you ever allowed yourself to be taught or shown something in the word of God that you have never heard anyone else talk about? Wait, you think this is impossible? I though you said you believe everything in the bible. Have you read the part of the scriptures where it said, things that are impossible with man is possible with God? I have already said, a finite mine will never see or understand some of the things in the word of God. They put limits on what they think the word of God is telling us. They think only what they read in the bible is what God is saying. God is saying a lot more than you think. After the transfiguring of Jesus, he went

down the mountain with his disciples. He then charged them to tell no man of what they had seen until after his resurrection from the dead. They wanted to know about Elijah. In some bibles it said, Jesus answered them saying, if you can receive this, Elijah has already come. Matthew 17: 11. And Jesus answered and said unto them, Elijah truly shall first come, and restore all things. 12. But I say unto you, that Elijah is come already, and they knew him not, but have done unto him whatsoever they listed. Likewise shall also the son of man suffer of them. 13. Then the disciples understood that he spake unto them of John the Baptist. Now are you saying that in the spirit, God can not take you back to those days, and show you in the spirit, what was happening at that time. If he can't, how can you have faith to believe, that one day he is coming back to receive you unto himself, that where he is we will be also. How is it that John was able to write the book of Revelation. He was in the present and wrote about the future. It was in the spirit and on the Lord's day, that John was given the things to write. He even wrote about the different lays of heaven. Hello, how's your faith now? If you can not receive this, than you probable don't believe that one day the trumpet will sound and the eyes of them that pierced Jesus in his side, when he come on the cloud, will see him also. Tell me this, how is it that all those from the beginning, to the day of the resurrection of Jesus, got to heaven? How is it that from the resurrection to the day of Jesus return, we are going to get to heaven? If you don't believe that in the spirit you can be taken and showing things in the word of God, how can you serve God in spirit and in truth? You must have faith to believe that all things are possible with God. In his word there are some things that we as pastors, (I am not a pastor) preachers, teachers, evangelist and apostle, will never be able to teach God people, if we can not trust and believe all of God words. Do we ever think about just how much the people of God are starving for more truth. Now please, don't misunderstand me, I am not that great teacher that you might think I am. I am limited to the things that I have learned in the word of God. I have heard some great spirit filled, let me say Holy Ghost filled preachers on the television. I do not know all of them by name but I am sure there are a lot more. More than I will ever know. But by name some are Creflo Dollars, John Hagen, Perry Stone, T D Jakes, Tony Edward and more. I am not leaving the women out because; I've seen some who can explain the scripture better than some men. I know this because what they are teaching are what I have been taught by the Holy Spirit and a few pastors. When you can agree with the word of God, and testify that what they are saying it's true according to the word of God, then your spirit can bear witness. Notice what I said, your spirit can bear witness, not your flesh. Only a child of the King can bear witness to the word of the King. Now just so you don't think that I don't know what I am talking about, I know the demons in the day of Jesus called him the son of David. It was not to bring glory unto God, but to in some way reveal him before his time and the scripture be fulfilled. Jesus knowing and recognizing the enemy in return told him or them to shut up and come out of the people they were in. In the old days, the Pharisees and Sadducees, who was a teacher of the law, thought they knew everything, realized too late that they were being taught by the teacher of teachers. They though they could tell people how to live and found out that the one they were teaching about in the word of law, was the word of

God. But in today time, because of the education that moms and dads want there children to learn about, will not save one soul. Children are sent to the best schools, if it is affordable, to get the best education possible to be able to climb, what some people call, the corporate ladder. Tell me this, can any of the schools today, who do not say, show or teach anything about Jesus; lead any of there student to the way of salvation. No, but they will in some way teach them that they don't have to forgive and love one another. I am not downing the school system, but just saying that children can pick up on things where teachers show them, and plant in their minds that they are better than someone else. This is not on the spiritual side, this is on the side of the enemy. God did not give his son for one group of people and the rest of the people die and go to hell. We all came from and through one man, Adam. No one is better than anyone else, because we all were conceived and shaped in the iniquity of sin. Everyone of us has fallen and come short of the glory of God. Your and my sin will not go unpunished. All of us must and will give in account for the way we treat other people. That's why I thank and always will thank God for his grace and mercy.

Now let me start with this one first to see if you can agree with it. Believe me, before I get finish, some will understand this and some will not, because just as the day of Pentecost, some could not believe people that was not of there culture, could speak there language. This one will be kind of simple. How many times have you heard that in the days of Noah that it rained forty days and forty night. Well I believe that because the bible said so, but that is not all that happen. Time after time from generation to generation, people have been told through out time, that it rained upon the earth forty days and forty nights. A lot of people could not read for themselves, so they really didn't know. They would only say and repeat what they heard the preacher say. This is one of the saying about children not being taught what God done in the life of men in the days of old. They will not learn that the world will not be destroyed with water anymore, but with fire. Schools do not teach this in the class rooms. Some churches will not teach this because, it has become unimportant to them. They are not worry about the soul of the people, but how much money they can raise. Believe me I am not talking about putting down tithes and offerings, because we must give ten percent of our earning back to God. But what I am talking about is, people today don't believe that Jesus could come anytime, at any day, or hour or minute or second. Just as the people of old did not believe Noah's preaching, it was going to rain, until it started to rain. You see, it had never rain before and they just could not take him at the word that was give to him by God. They had never seen it before and if you could talk to the ones who seen this, they would say yes it did. Shocker, all of the flood water did not fall from the sky, or heaven. That's why you must study for yourself. Yes it did you say: ok lets go to bible school. In Genesis 7: 10 it say's. In the six hundredth year of Noah's life, in the second month, the seventeenth day of the month, the same day were all the fountains of the great deep broken up, and the windows of heaven were opened. (the same day were all the fountains of the great deep broken up). Some of the flood came up out of the earth, out of the sea. Remember the entire earth was covered by water before God separated them. The people in the day of Ezekiel believed it when God spoke to Tyre. (Ezekiel 26:19). After forty days and night of raining and fountains coming up, God stopped it and the rain from heaven was restrained. Now has anyone ever taught this to you in vocational bible school, or you just didn't go? They can't teach what they don't know. You're read it and so did I, but it was not revealed unto me until the Holy Spirit showed it unto me. (and he shall teach you all things and bring all things to your remembrance, whatsoever I have said unto you). Some will never learn because they will never surrender all unto the Holy Spirit. He, meaning the Holy Spirit can teach and show you things that no man could. He is the one and only true witness on this earth since Jesus has gone back to sit on the right hand of the Father. He show and teaches us more about Jesus than we could ever imagine. As long as we are looking at things through the physical though, we will never have the mine of Jesus Christ. So let this mind be in you, which was also in Christ Jesus. Other wise you might not ever have the relationship with Christ that you think you have, or see what he is trying to show you.

Moving on to another point to see if you can see this one. This one you have read also. Maybe you have put it together by letting the Holy Spirit revealed it unto you. In St. John 19, the scripture speaks of a man born blind from birth. The disciples question Jesus about sin, who committed it, him or his parents. Jesus responded by saying neither him or his parents, but that the works of God should be made manifest in him. Jesus them tells them that he must do the work of him that sent him, (meaning his Father), while it is day: (while he was on the earth at that time) the night cometh, (when he would leave earth) when no man can work. (those who don't know him can do nothing to glorify the Father). Verse 5. As long as I am in the world, I am the light of the world. Getting straight to the point, in verse six, what did Jesus do. 6. When he had thus spoken, he spat on the ground, and made clay of the spittle, and he anointed the eyes of the blind man with the clay. What did he really do? Are you really spiritual enough to see this? Have you allowed the Holy Spirit to reveal it to you? If you haven't, than maybe you are not as spiritual as you think. How can you read your bible every day and not allow the Holy Spirit to teach you? Have I made my point yet? We need more than just wisdom and knowledge to understand things about God. When I realized what was said about the enemy Satan, how subtle he is, I start praying to God for spiritual wisdom, spiritual knowledge and spiritual understanding of his word. Thank God he is a God of his word, ask and it shall be given unto you. Ask and you shall receive, knot and it shall be open, seek and ye shall find. He answered my pray, this don't mean I know everything because I do not. I don't know as much or even pretend to know and understand everything. It just that, when I pray and read, I meditate on what I have read, the Holy Spirit reveal some things to me that I can't see with the carnal mind. God is not a selfish God, he will do the same for you if you give him enough of your time in seeking him, to see what it is he want you to do. So what did Jesus do? He done nothing new in this case or any other. The only new thing that was done was that the Holy Spirit, over came Mary, and she gave birth to the son of God. That's why nothing else is important or more important than Jesus. It is all about him and nothing else on this earth matter but love and Jesus. Jesus is love. Remember Solomon said in Ecclesiastes, 12: 7. Then shall the dust return to the earth as it was: and the spirit shall return unto God who gave it. 8. Vanity of vanities, said the preacher; all is vanity. There is nothing new under the sun. So what did Jesus do. When he bent down and spat on the ground, he was not along. Yes he was you said, I think not. Remember when he was baptized by John, Jesus went up straightway out of the water: and lo, the heavens were opened unto him, and he saw the Spirit of God descending like a dove, and lighting upon him. (Matthew 4:16). To me it was the Holy Spirit. Then remember what Jesus said when Philip said, Lord show us the Father. John 14: 11. Believe me that I am in the Father, and the Father in me; or else believe me for the very works' sake. Plus I and my Father are one. All three were there, just as all three were there when God said, let us make man in our image, after our likeness. Genesis 2: 7. And the Lord God formed man of the dust of the ground, and breathed into his nostrils the breath of life; and man became a living soul. Jesus use what the man was made from. Man was made from the dust of the earth, and there was a mist that watered the whole earth. From the mist that watered the whole earth, when God made man the earth was already moisture. (Genesis 2: 6). I pray and hope that you under stand that the earth was without sin when man was made. There was no need to wet the dust because of the mist watering the earth. But when Jesus spit the earth it was filled with sin. So Jesus used spittle to make the dust moisture and anointed it, putting the clay on the eyes of the man that was born blind from birth. Then he said unto the man, go wash in the pool of Siloam and he did. The man therefore went and washed and came back seeing. (Ok here's another example) and then you will have to seek and trust the Holy Spirit to reveal more unto you. But I warn you that you must pray and wait for your answer from God. Do not rush to get an answer because the enemy can and will deceive you if you are not patience enough to wait on the Lord. Remember the enemy has made a promise to God that he would (Exodus 15: 9) I will pursue, I will overtake, I will divide the spoil; my lust shall be satisfied up on them; I will draw my sword, my hand shall destroy them. Spoken through an angry king of Egypt by the name of Pharaoh. That's why Saul who name was change to Paul warned the Ephesians to put on the whole armor of God, that ye may be able to stand against the whiles of the devil. We are not wrestling against flesh and blood, but against principalities, against powers, against the rulers of the darkness of this world, against spiritual wickedness in high places. Wherefore take unto you the whole armor of God, that ye may be able to withstand in the evil day, and having done all to stand. Girt your loins with truth, put on the breastplate of righteousness, shod your feet with the preparation of the gospel of peace, taking the shield of faith that ye may be able to quench all the fiery darts of the wicked, put on the helmet of salvation and the sword of the Spirit which is the word of God. Then pray for all saints with supplication in the Spirit and watch with perseverance and supplication. That is why we must be aware to what is going on around us as much as possible. That we can not see, we must trust and depend on God for his protection. Sometime and a lot of the times, the enemy can use or persuade us in doing thing that we think is right. Sometimes we can do things out of kindness or what we feel and call love. But you see, we all must be kind and graceful that the enemy can not pull the, in our terms, wool over the eyes of God. God do not have that small infinite mind that man has. He is God and he sees and knows all things. That's another reason why we fall short, most can only believe what they see and a very, very little of what they hear. The enemy told Eve that she would not die if she ate of the tree of knowledge, good and evil. She will become as gods, knowing good and evil, but she would not die. He was wrong in saying she would not die, spiritual they did. Becoming gods he use part of the truth, we are gods. Psalm 82:6 I have said, Ye are gods; and all of you are children of the most High. John 10:34. Jesus answered them, Is it not written in your law, I said, Ye are gods? So she gave to her husband and he ate and they were both separated from God in the spiritual way. The enemy had tricked and defeated mankind in separating them from God. His plan was on the way to destroy man, that he would never enter back into heaven to live with God. Why am I writing all this you might ask? It need to be made as plain as possible before I ask and explain my next question. You must believe and understand that when Jesus return to receive the church unto himself, it must be spotless. There must not be any sin in the church, because sin can't dwell in the present of God the Father. That's why Jesus sinless blood had to be shed. When God the Father looks at us, he looks at us through the blood of his son and sees us without sin. Thank God for his grace and mercy. Here is the big question. What would have happen if Mary would have touched Jesus, after he had risen from the grave, before going to his Father? Back up scripture said that when she went to touch him, he told her not to touch him because he had not ascended unto his Father. I pray you haven't forgotten what the enemy promise God. He had already beguiled Eve in the garden and now he was trying to pull that same old trick. I must say again, you will not see this if you are looking through physical eyes and with a carnal mind. He is still on his mission to steal, kill and destroy. He will do anything in his power to destroy mankind in any way that he can. He will use your husband, your wife, your sons and daughter, friends or whosoever. The only thing we have to overcome, and in rejecting the enemy, is Jesus. God gave Adam instruction not to eat from the tree in the mist of the garden. The only one that he could not eat from was the tree of knowledge, of good and evil. The day that thou eat of that tree thou shall surely die. (Genesis 2:17). Now the enemy, knowing that he would not be able to persuade Adam, so he went to the weaker one, woman. Because he was able to trick the woman in beguiling her, the enemy told her, she would not die. He said that God knew that if she ate thereof, their eyes shall be opened and ye shall be as gods, knowing good and evil. Now the Lord told Adam not to eat of the tree and in the conversation between the enemy and Eve, she said, God hath said, ye shall not eat of it, neither shall ye touch it, lest ye die. (Genesis 3:3) Remember the word touch. Mary Magdalene whom Jesus had cast seven demons out of, was the same Mary who went to the sepulcher.(Mark 16:9). When he clean or cast the demons out of her, he didn't give her a body like that of himself: when he had risen from the grave. He had to be the first to be raised from the grave, making a sinless and prefect way back to the Father. That body she was in, was still of sin nature, and it had to be returned back to the dust, from which it came. Now she did not know all the tricks of the enemy but God did. The enemy tried to find and kill Jesus when he was a baby and God the Father protected him through his servant Joseph. God used his angel to warn Joseph through a dream to take the child and his mother and take them into the land of Egypt until the death of Herod, so the scripture be fulfilled that was spoken by the prophet. Out of Egypt have I called my son.(Matthew 2:11-23). Now again through Mary without her knowing what she was doing, Satan, the devil, tried to contaminate, or destroy our way back into the kingdom of God. If she had touched him, being born and shaped in the iniquity of sin, where demons also live in sin, the enemy would have stained the plans of God. But knowing what he was trying to do, knowing his tricks, knowing his threat, knowing his wickedness, before he could use Mary in his sinful sin skills, Jesus responded and told Mary not to touch him. I also know he was telling her not to cling onto him. Now I know there are some out there who will say this is not in the bible, who will never see this or agree with it. Those are the ones who can't see because they are so use to seeing with the carnal mind. It is in the bible and the bible back it up. Watch this if you think it is not. Jesus was in the stage of completing the narrow and sinless way back to the kingdom, he was going away to prepare a place for those who accept and love him. Mary was reaching out of love in a different body form. She was in the form of sin and iniquity. That could not go to the present of God the Father, because he is a Holy, pure and spotless God. The only way back to him is through his son Jesus. Jesus is not the sinful way back to the Father but he is the sinless way. He is not the crocked way, but the straight and narrow way. He is not the part time when I want you or need you, but the full time keeper of our salvation. He is not the half true but the full and only true son of God. He didn't speak lies but spoke the only truth about the kingdom of heaven, because he is the only and first one to leave heaven, be born, die and return back from the dead, to sit on the right side of the Father. If you still don't understand let me show you another way. Maybe some of you has never read or heard of an scapegoat. The priest, Aaron had to wash and prepare himself before he would go before God to sprinkle blood from the animals on the mercy seat. If he had not, he would have been killed. He had to go through the instructions of God in getting ready to enter the Holy of Holiness. Even his attire that he wore into the present of God had to be holy. Yes God even gave him instruction on how to dress before entering into his presence. He would have to wash himself before putting on the Holy attire to go before God. If he wouldn't have washed his body, that would have also made him unclean and God would have struck him dead. No man could be in the tabernacle, when the priest went into it or touch him in any way. That would have put a sin spot on Aaron and God would have seen it. It's all in Leviticus chapter sixteen, read it. Jesus is the scapegoat for you and I. When God the father looks at us, he sees us through the blood of the lamb, which is Jesus, his one and only son. Jesus is the lamb who was offered to sit on the mercy seat on the right side of God in heaven. Now read Revelation chapter five. Now let me back up to finish clearing up my point. Hopefully we all know that Jesus did not have an earthly father but an heavenly Father. Joseph was called his father by many people because they can't believe and accept the fact that things that are impossible with man, is possible with God. I know there are some who said that, if she would have touched him nothing would have happen. What happen when the woman with the issue of blood for twelve long years touched not his body, but the hem of his garment or clothes. She touched him out of desperation and fear. Even though her faith is not spoken of, but her belief, because she said, if I may touch but his clothes: I shall be whole. (Mark 5:25-34). Oh how I wish we as christians had this type of faith and belief in the word of

God. There are so many people in the church and world today, who believe in so many things, but have a very hard time believing in the word of God. All those people and his disciples were touching and bumping up against Jesus, had no affect on him. Just like the word of God has no affect on a lot of people who has no respect for God. You say yes it does: than tell me this: why is it that so many people can go into the sanctuary today, raise so much cane, when it is supposed to be set aside for worship, not fussing, cursing and causing confusion? How is it that you can sit there and watch your child write on the back of the pews. Some eat candy and throw the paper on the floor and leave it there, what's wrong with your purse or pocket? Some spill drinks on the pews and you don't try to get it up. This is not just the children doing this, but it's some parents also. Your children do it because they see you do it and you let them do it. They can not put there foot on your coffee table and they bet not spill any kind of drink on the sofa. Then why do you let them do it in the house of the Lord. There is a lot of ways you can look at this statement. God will not dwell in an unclean temple. Now I know that he is talking about the body. What if God would cause pain to run through your body when this is going on., I bet he will get some attention then. Getting back to the woman at hand. But when this woman came with expectance, expecting a healing, she received it because of her faith. When she touched his cloth, he immediately knew that virtue had left his body. Here is something else you probably overlooked also, when the virtue went out of his body (it) turned him about in the press, and he said, Who touched my clothes? Now his disciples didn't understand what had happen, so they complained and ask him to look around to see all the people around him. How could he ask a question like this? (Just let me throw this in and I hope it will help someone realize something. The church is body members. These were the body members and they were the church, with the word. It's unknown how many was at church and none of them came expecting the way this woman did. She came expecting a healing and got it because she came expecting something form God. How beautiful it would be, if the members of the church today had enough faith to come expecting a healing from the word of God when it is preached. The names on the sick list on your church program would dwindle, and more testimonies would be given, on how good God really is, if they came with the right heart and expecting a healing from God). Jesus didn't respond to them but looked through what they were saying: because something that they didn't understand, had just happen. So as he looked to see the woman, she knowing what had just taken place, came out of fear trembling, fell down at his feet and told Jesus of all the trouble she had been having for twelve long years. Hey, hey, hey, what's wrong with this picture? Do you see it or has it ever come to your attention? This woman was out of place, and if it had been know of by the men following Jesus, there would have been an uproar to have her taken outside the city to be stone, because she was consider unclean. All that she touched and all that touched her would have been considered unclean. In response Jesus called her daughter, and told her, thy faith hath made thee whole; go in peace and be whole of thy plague. Now let me try explaining why it was a sin for her to touch Jesus. Jesus was and is the one and only true righteous sacrifice that could, would, and be except by God the Father. Now this may be a little heavy for some of those who don't read there bibles enough to know this. In the days of old, and he was living in those days, it was a sin for a woman to enter into the sanctuary. If a woman gave birth, to a male or female child, she was not permitted to even touch anything hollowed, nor come into the sanctuary, until the days of her purifying be fulfilled. She could not have anything to do with the things of God, until after her blood flow dried up. Then she still couldn't entered into the sanctuary until she would bring a sin offering to the door of the tabernacle of the congregation unto the priest. The priest would then take her sin offering, make an atonement for her, and then she would be cleaned from her blood issues. This can be found in the laws.(Leviticus chapter 12). Men don't fool yourself, men could not enter into the sanctuary either if there was any type of fluid flowing from his body. He also was consider unclean and had to go through the same steps of that for a woman. Everything he or she would touch, sit on, wear or lay upon was consider under clean.

Now for those who like to eat pink or red meat, that is a sin also. (Genesis 9: 4). But flesh with the life thereof, which is the blood thereof, shall ye not eat. (Deuteronomy 12:23). Only be sure that thou eat not the blood: for the blood is the life; and thou mayest not eat the life with the flesh. It was the body of Jesus that was beaten, and blood shaded that we must eat and drink. (Matthew 26:26). And as they were eating, Jesus took bread, and blessed it, and brake it, and gave it to the disciples, and said, Take, eat; this is my body. 27. And he took the cup, and gave thanks, and gave it to them, saying, Drink ye all of it. (1 Corinthians 11: 23-30) this do in remembrance of me. That's the only blood that is righteous to be drink, that of Jesus. So see when the woman touched Jesus, he knew. He also knew the word, because he is the word of God, which became flesh. That's why it is so important that we not have women handling the Lord Supper or teaching, when they are in the time of being unclean. The women of old was not allowed to have anything to do with the holiness of God doing there uncleanness time. A woman who is standing as pastor, should step down, not from pastoring, but at that time, have someone else to deliver the word of God to the congregation. But because we pick and choose that what we want and overlook that which would cut and convict us. If we say we believe all of the word of God, that should not be. That's why it is better to obey all of God words than the thoughts of man, what he thinks we should do. Now if they don't know this, it should be taught by the pastor of the church and I hope you know what it said in Ezekiel 34:2 about the pastor not feeding God flock. I know we think we live in a different world, under a different set of rules, but God still has not changed. I know we are under grace and God still has mercy, but God still has not changed. God can't be a lie because he is the truth. He don't have a spot on him because that would make him imperfect, and he is prefect. He always has been, and always will be. That's why Mary could not touch Jesus, the church must be presented prefect to dwell with a perfect GOD. The body of Christ was headed straight back to heaven to sprinkle his blood on the mercy seat. The body of Mary was still flesh and had not been changed, but Christ had been changed. He is and was that straight and narrow way back to the father. That's why he was able to walk through the walls or door and Mary still had to use the door. He had to present the church back to his Father in a prefect and spotless way. The way; Jesus is the way, back to the Father, must be and remain sinless and prefect. Satan lose again and the victory is ours, through Jesus, the prefect and sinless son of God the Father. Mary did not knows but, glory to our Father, he knew and knows all the tricks of the enemy, who wants us all to die and go to hell with him. But God said, not so.

GOD BLESS and stay prayed up.

Printed in the United States
By Bookmasters